A LIVELY APPROACH TO BASIC ENGLISH SKILLS

ON YOUR MARKS

PAUL GROVES

JOHN GRIFFIN

NIGEL GRIMSHAW

BOOK 1

Self-marking chart

Copy out this chart and fill it in after you have finished each section in this book.

Section title	
Funny or serious?	
Fact or fiction? (for stories and plays)	
How much did I like it? (mark 1–10)	
New words learnt	
What was the hardest thing to do?	
What was the easiest thing to do?	
How many marks do I give myself? (out of 10)	

Contents

1 The Tompkins at breakfast

Cast

Mr Tompkins Mrs Tompkins Anne-Marie Nigel

Scene: The Tompkins' dining room

Mr Tompkins	Where is it?
Mrs Tompkins	What?
Mr Tompkins	My bacon.
Mrs Tompkins	I don't feel like cooking it.
Mr Tompkins	But you always cook my bacon.
Mrs Tompkins	Well, I've had enough. You cook it.
Mr Tompkins	Me!
Mrs Tompkins	You should help around the house.
Mr Tompkins	It's woman's work.
Mrs Tompkins	Well, let it be man's work for a change.
Mr Tompkins	I'm not cooking. What would my mates say?
Mrs Tompkins	Lots of men cook. What about the chefs at posh hotels?
Mr Tompkins	You cook it, Anne-Marie.
Anne-Marie	I don't want my new dress splashed with fat.
Mrs Tompkins	Wear an apron.
Anne-Marie	No, I'll smell of frying. Ted my boyfriend won't like that.
Mrs Tompkins	None of you mind if I smell of frying.
Mr Tompkins	You'll just have to do it.
Mrs Tompkins	I'm not doing it. I'm sick of this family. I want a rest.
Nigel	I'll do it.
Mrs Tompkins	Oh, no! I'm not having that. Remember the Christmas pudding.
Nigel	I didn't know the oven would blow up like that.
Mrs Tompkins	There's still some on the ceiling.
Mr Tompkins	Well, if you won't let him do it, you'll have to.
Mrs Tompkins	I'm not. I'm having a rest. It's time you took your turn.
Mr Tompkins	Well, I put my foot down. Nigel, you do it. I'm starving.
Nigel	Okay, Dad. (*He goes out and comes back quickly.*)
Mr Tompkins	That was quick.
Nigel	It doesn't matter who cooks the bacon now.
Mr Tompkins	Why not?
Nigel	The dog's eaten it.

Make up a play

Make up a play about a quarrel at breakfast when things go wrong. It could be your family, or you could make up a family.

Before you start, look and see how the play about the Tompkins is set out. Set out your play like the Tompkins play. It could begin like this:

Mum	What would you like for breakfast?
John	I don't want any breakfast.
Mum	Why not? You must have breakfast.

Describing people

1 Write two sentences that describe Mr Tompkins.
2 Write two sentences that describe Anne-Marie.

Making sentences

Write this out in four sentences. Put in four capital letters and four full-stops:

i like sausages best my brother likes crispy bacon my sister will only have a piece of toast she is worried about her figure

Capital letters

Write out the name of a posh hotel. Begin each word with a capital letter.

Drawing

Draw the oven blowing up with the Christmas pudding in it. Or you could draw the dog stealing the bacon.

Spelling

Use each of these words in a sentence of your own:

having   ceiling   starving   frying

Note: There is no *e* before the *ing*

Let's talk about breakfast

1 Who should get the breakfast when both parents go out to work?
2 Why do doctors say you need to start the day with a good breakfast?
3 What must you do if the frying pan or chip pan catches fire?
4 What do you like for breakfast? Copy this menu card and then write out your own breakfast menu. It could be for your posh hotel.

Breakfast Menu

Fruit juices
Grapefruit segments

**

Porridge
Various cereals

**

Bacon, egg, sausage
Scrambled eggs
Boiled egg
Kippers

**

Toast and marmalade or jam

**

Tea or coffee

---

2 Cooper

Tommy had a dream. He wanted to do magic and he wanted to be famous. When he was a small boy he read books about magic. He bought magic tricks and invented tricks of his own.

When he grew up, his act was perfect. He had magic rings joined together. When he touched them with his wand they fell apart. He tied a knot in a rope and cut through the knot. When he shook the rope the knot vanished and the rope was in one piece. He did card tricks too. He made glasses of water vanish. He waved his empty hand, and at once it held a bunch of flowers.

He did his tricks for his family. They said he was very good. But Tommy wanted more than that. He wanted to show his tricks to crowds of people.

One night it was talent night at a local hall. Tommy went along with his bag of magic tricks. He waited for his turn. He began to feel very scared. He felt even more scared when he went on stage.

His first tricks went wrong. His magic rings didn't fall apart. Someone laughed. He dropped the rings on the floor and quickly began his second trick. That failed too. Nothing went right. Everybody was helpless with laughter. Tommy felt awful. He finished his act and left the stage.

Tommy told the manager of the hall that he was very sorry. He would never try to do magic on stage again. But the manager only laughed. He said it was a wonderful act. He had never seen anything so funny. He wanted Tommy to work at the hall every night.

Tommy Cooper stopped being scared on stage. He could have done all his magic tricks properly. But he made them all go wrong. His hopeless act made him famous all over the world.

ut

from these mixed-up

glasses of water He
nted than Tommy But
tricks wrong

he story means:
n_ _ _ _ _
out of sight'?

f_ _ _ _ _

3

Ev
thi

Cop
mar
yello

True or false?

Which sentences are true? Write them down.
1 Tommy wanted to be a footballer.
2 Tommy wanted to be famous.
3 He made jugs of water vanish.
4 He made glasses of water vanish.
5 His first tricks on stage went well.
6 His first tricks on stage went wrong.

Capital letters

Names begin with a capital letter. Write these out correctly.

tommy cooper   mandy brown
indra patel   errol gomes
dawn wade   joel garner
nikos kouskas

Missing letters

Write these sentences out. Put in the missing letters.
1 He did magic tri__s.
2 The house was built of bri__s.
3 She began to li__ the ice-cream.
4 He ate so much that he felt si__.
5 The dog ran after the sti__.

Sort these c

Write sentences
words.
1 vanish made
2 more that wa
3 went first His

Words

What word from t
1 'thought up'?
2 'disappear, go
    v_____
3 'went wrong'?

The yellow page

Everything on this page is about the colour yellow. Read this riddle first, and write down your answer.

WHAT AM I?

My first is in apple
But not in pear.
My second's in ladder
But not in stair.
My third is in moon
But not in sun.
My fourth is in bomb
But not in gun.
My last's in minute
But not in hour.
My whole, if you suck me,
Is very sour.

Copy out all the words you can find in this grid. (Do not look in the book.) Can you find any words that are not yellow? Which word is put in twice?

S	J	D	A	F	F	O	D	I	L	C	G
X	C	P	U	B	W	V	T	A	B	C	R
X	Z	A	T	Q	N	P	A	O	Y	D	A
C	R	N	R	P	Z	U	M	O	O	N	P
U	Q	C	H	E	E	S	E	C	L	E	E
S	P	A	X	Y	D	J	V	W	K	F	F
T	A	K	E	M	A	M	B	E	R	G	R
A	O	E	L	N	A	G	O	L	D	H	U
R	Z	C	A	N	A	R	Y	E	I	U	I
D	K	N	W	S	H	S	F	G	T	H	T
X	A	F	N	M	C	U	S	T	A	R	D
B	G	X	O	R	B	D	M	L	I	J	K

5 words = good   8 or more = very good

difference?

l from these pairs in
ur own:

stare   our hour

entences

e words you found in
 to write three
your own. Can you put
vords into one sentence?

k about night and

o you like best about night?
o you not like about it?
d early man see the sun as

does the sun rise in your

does it set?

a
c

I'l

arc
he
on
he
'I
H
to h

It
unde
the sl
of the
I sh
Dogs o
An old
But th
shouted
Savage!'

I felt
went a
shoutir
notice.
Mos
I'll ev

10

Read this poem and think of a name for it. Notice that lines of poetry do not have to rhyme.

The sun comes up out of its deep hole in space
Trailing drops of molten gold
The moon comes out of a sea of stars
In a ring of silver
But I am a poet
I love the night
I love silver
I am not a slave to the sun and its golden bribes

Make a list

What colour do you like most? Make a list of the things you own in that colour.

Do you know?

Answer in sentences:
1 What colour is a grapefruit before it is yellow?
2 Name three things that are always yellow.
3 What are you if you are 'yellow'?
4 What phone book has 'Yellow' in its title?
5 Write a word that rhymes with 'yellow'.
6 What colours do you think yellow clashes with?

A poem

Write a sun or moon poem. You can use some of the words in the poem above if you like. It does not have to rhyme.

What is the

Write each word
a sentence of yo

son sun   stair
whole hole

Write in se

Use any of th
the word grid
sentences of
two of the w

Let's tall
the sun

1 What d
2 What d
3 Why di
  a god?
4 Where
  area?
5 Where

4 A quiet swim

I had been hunting and rolling in things. It was a hot
ay. I went for a quiet swim and a drink. The river is
eep there, by the small landing stage. I was just
paddling about lazily. I heard the boys before I saw
them.

There were two of them. They came down to the
landing stage. The smaller one suddenly shouted, 'Look!
That dog! It's drowning!'

I looked round. I couldn't see another dog.

'No, it isn't,' the other boy said. 'It's all right.'

'It's drowning,' the first one repeated. 'Here, boy, here!
l save you.' He seemed quite excited.

Then I realised that he was talking to me. I swam
und faster. I wanted to show him that I was safe. But
ran off and came back with a long branch. He stood
the landing stage and held out the long branch. Was
going to throw it? Did he want me to fetch it?
Here, boy, here!' he shouted. 'Grab it! I'll pull you in.'
e beat it on the water. I drew back. I didn't want it
it me. He reached out further with it. Then he fell in.

was lucky for him that I was there. He went right
r the water. As he came up again, I grabbed him by
irt and towed him to the bank. He scrambled out
water. He was dripping wet. I got out too.
ok myself and waited for the words of praise.
ften get medals for saving people from drowning.
sheep dog friend of mine told me that.
he boy was very angry. 'Stupid animal!' he
. His friend was laughing. 'He's savage, too.
he went on. 'He grabbed me in his teeth.'

hurt. But a dog can't argue with a boy. So I just
way. It seemed the wisest thing to do. He was still
g and he threw something after me. I took no

t of the time I like human beings. But I don't think
er understand them.

Write in sentences

1 Imagine you are a fish swimming in a river. Write four or five sentences about what you see.
2 Write one sentence about each of these:
   – When you have been misunderstood about something.
   – When you have been in danger.
   – When you have helped somebody who didn't want help.

Find out

What each of these mean:

dogleg   dog paddle   dogsbody
dog-tired   doghouse

Making sentences

Write this in six sentences. Use six capital letters and six full-stops:

my mistress is very cruel she does not feed me every day i have to look for scraps in dustbins you can see my bones sticking out she sometimes locks me out i am often beaten with a stick

Spelling

Use each of these words in a sentence of your own:

lazily   repeated   realised   throw
praise   friend   something

Make a list

Make a list of things you need for a dog or cat.

Let's talk about dogs

1 What do you think it would be like to be a dog?
2 How important would smells be?
3 What would you really think of your owner?
4 What animal would you like to be for a day?

5 Cyclists should be seen and not hurt

Mind that bike!

True or false?

1 Look at the pictures. Choose the best ending for the sentence below, then write out the whole sentence.

This poster was made
(a) to make people laugh.
(b) to warn drivers to look out for cyclists.
(c) to warn cyclists not to bang into cars.

2 Write out the sentences that are true. There is one true sentence about each picture.

Picture A
The cyclist has gone through both windows of the car.
The car was signalling to go right.

Picture B
The driver has turned right without noticing the cyclist.
The car is on the wrong side of the road.

Picture C
The car has cut across the cyclist without noticing him.
The cyclist was not looking where he was going.

Picture D
The driver should have looked in his mirror first.
The cyclist did not notice the car.

Your own poster

Make a poster for one of these safety rules:

Make sure young children can't get into the street.
Keep dogs on leads in the street.
Use car seat belts.

Let's talk about jobs in the home

Here are two facts about the pictures.

Both ladies are carrying shopping. Both drivers are men.

Copy out this form and fill in the answers.

Questions	Answers
In your house, who usually does these things:	
1 Makes the meals?	
2 Washes the dishes?	
3 Dries the dishes?	
4 Washes the clothes?	
5 Drives the car? (on a family drive)	
6 Gets up first?	
7 Locks the door at night?	
8 Deals with the bills?	
9 Has first look at the newspaper?	
10 Tells off the children?	
11 Cleans the car?	
12 Makes the beds?	

6 The missing frisby

It was a very hot day, and we were playing in the park. Sue threw the frisby to Dave and Dave missed it. We haven't seen that frisby since.

Oh, it didn't just vanish at once. It floated down on to the path. Dave went to get it, when something happened. A small brown dog with a fluffy tail came from nowhere and ran off with the frisby. We thought at first that the dog wanted a game. But it ran straight out of the park and down a street of small houses. We all went after it, as fast as we could run. We just saw it go into one of the houses. When we got there, the front door was open but everything was very quiet. There was no dog, and no frisby. Dave shouted, 'Anyone home?'

The only reply was a groaning noise from indoors. We didn't know what to do. Then Sue marched in, and we all followed her.

We found old Mr Harper alone on the floor in the back kitchen. He had fallen off his painting ladder. Paint was running down the wall. He couldn't move much, but he told Sue to fetch the next-door neighbour, Mrs Wilson. Mrs Wilson came in and rang for the ambulance. Then she made Mr Harper a cup of tea. She asked us why we were in the house. Sue told her about the dog.

'What dog?' said Mrs Wilson. We all looked at each other. Where was it? 'Mr Harper doesn't have a dog any more,' she told us. 'What did it look like?'

'Funny,' she said when we told her, 'He did have a dog a bit like that, called Rex. Poor thing got run over about five weeks ago.'

I had a very creepy feeling just then. We all did. Mrs Wilson let Sue have a good look all over the house. It was no good, there was no dog. Then the ambulance came for Mr Harper.

We never saw that frisby again either.

Sentence endings

Finish these sentences. Look at the story again to help you.

1 We thought that the dog wanted a game but ....
2 When we got to the house ....
3 Mr Harper had ....
4 Mrs Wilson asked us ....
5 Mrs Wilson said that Rex ....

How, what and who?

Answer each question in one short sentence.

1 How do you play with a frisby?
2 What two things do you find in most kitchens?
3 Who uses a ladder for his work?

Capital letters

1 Names begin with capital letters. Write these out correctly:

dave   sue   mrs wilson   mr harper

2 Write out the names of four of your friends.
3 Write out the names of four adults you know.

Write in sentences

Think about this. You go alone into a house and find an old person. He or she is hurt. There is no one else in the house. Write four sentences to say what you would do to help him, or her.

Let's talk about helping people

Compare your sentences with the others in the class. Then talk about these questions:

What is the first thing to do to help the old person?
What should you do next?
What are the things you should *not* do?

7 Supper

The other night I met a man
Who went to sea in an old Coke can.
With a great big smile he left the shore
Using a lolly stick as an oar.

The other night I met a dog
Whose body was made of a chocolate log.
Instead of eyes he had Smarties.
Not two but enough for a thousand parties.

The other night I met a spider
Who drank a glass of sparkling cider.
At the end of each long leg
Was a Cadbury's creme-filled egg.

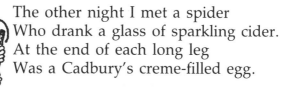

I told my Mum about my dreams.
She said; 'It's eating custard creams
Just before you go to bed.'
So I ate a lump of cheese instead.

The dream I had that night was worse.
I saw myself inside a hearse.
The driver was a sharp-toothed rat.
And round my coffin flew a bat.

I now have just a cup of tea.
I find I sleep most peacefully.
Something deep inside my head.
Wants my stomach to rest in bed.

Missing letters

All these words begin with the same letters. Can you write them?
1 What 'Can' is a country? Can___
2 What 'can' is a sweet? can__
3 What 'can' can you light? can___
4 What 'can' is a gun? can___
5 What 'can' can you boat in? can__
6 What 'can' is a bird? can___

Dream sentences

There is one wrong word in each sentence. Write them out correctly.
1 The man trotted down the road on his bike.
2 The tortoise sprinted up the path.
3 The sailor put the telescope to his ear.
4 Gran sawed me a new blouse.
5 Mum polished the coal in the grate.
6 Dad lit the electric cooker.

Rhymes

What other words rhyme with:

man   dog   bed   rat   tea

Write in sentences

Write four sentences about each of these 'dreams':
1 Being at sea in a shoe.
2 Eating a meal that gets bigger as you eat it.
3 Being chased by a big spider.

Drawing

Draw a picture to go with the poem.

A dream meeting

Who or what, could you meet in a dream? Write four sentences about your meeting. You could start with one of these beginnings:

The other night I met a ....
The other morning I met a ....
The other afternoon I met a ....

Let's talk about dreams

1 Talk about your last dream. Was it happy or sad? Did it frighten you? Did you wake up?
2 What food makes you dream?

8 The tree

Tracy sat on the wall. She was angry. Her brother Warren and his friends were playing up in the tree like monkeys. They were shouting, trying to climb past each other. Tracy wanted to climb too, but Warren said no. He and the others shook the lower branches to stop her. It was too dangerous, they said. Tracy shouted at them all, jumped off the wall, and went home feeling very cross.

Next day she came home from school alone. She stopped by the tree. She stood for some time looking at it. Then she put her bag on the wall and began to climb.

The first branches were thick and easy. But she was smaller than any of the boys. It was hard work. After a while she looked down. The ground was a long way below her. She felt scared and stopped. She was safe here. Perhaps Warren was right. She was too little. She was only a girl.

That made her angry! She looked up again. The green shadows and moving light tempted her on. She held very tight to each branch. She placed her feet carefully. Up she went.

At last she stopped again. She was high up now. The branches were thin, but she held on to the trunk of the tree. The tree-top moved gently in the wind, but she wasn't frightened. From here she could see everything. She could see the red roofs of the houses, and the shining river, and the cars on the main road. She felt brave and strong. She felt like a bird. It was great. Then, very slowly, she climbed down again.

At home, she said nothing about climbing the tree. She knew it would only get her into trouble. Later that evening, she went back to the tree with Warren and the boys. But she didn't even try to join in. She sat on the wall and watched them messing about in the tree. Nothing showed on her round, red face. But inside she smiled, and remembered.

Look at the story again

Answer in sentences:
1 When the story begins, where was Tracy sitting?
2 When she tried to climb the tree, how did the boys stop her?
3 Why was it harder for her than the boys?
4 What could she see from the top of the tree?
5 Why didn't she tell Warren or her parents about climbing the tree?

Spelling

These words have four letters. The last two letters are always the same. Write out the words.
1 This makes your hair neat. c _ _ _
2 This blows things up. b _ _ _
3 A branch, an arm or a leg is this. l _ _ _
4 When you can't feel you are this. n _ _ _

Write in sentences

Have you ever done something rather dangerous? When? Where? Did you hurt yourself? Write five sentences about what happened.

Let's talk about doing dangerous things

1 Why did Tracy climb the tree? Did she think she could do it safely? Did everyone think she could do it? What do you think about what she did?
2 Is it brave or silly to do things like mountain-climbing, motor-racing or hang-gliding?

9 Lions

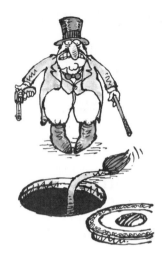

Read this true story that happened in Birmingham in 1889.

Nearly all the people of Birmingham went to the Onion Fair. There was something for everybody. There were rides, shows, competitions and good food. In 1889 Mr Bostock's circus was part of the fair. But not many people were going to see it.

Suddenly there was a cry, 'Lions loose!' The crowds ran for shelter. In fact only one lion had escaped. He quickly ran through the crowds and was lost. There were soon rumours* that lions were tearing people to pieces. Everybody was very frightened.

Mr Bostock quickly got a canvas-covered wagon. He drove through the streets until he came to a sewer* near Aston brook. He shouted to the crowd to be quiet. He looked into the sewer. He said lions always hid in the nearest sewer. Mr Bostock backed the wagon up to the entrance. He went into the tunnel. He carried a gun and stick. There were pistol shots, screams and roars. Then the trapdoor of the wagon closed. Mr Bostock pulled the canvas off the wagon. There was the lion, in a cage. Mr Bostock bowed and the crowd cheered.

Mr Bostock's circus was full up for the next week. Everybody wanted to see the lion that had frightened the city. Nobody seemed to notice that it was an old, sleepy lion. In fact, the lion on show was no more dangerous than a cat. It had been in the wagon all the time. Mr Bostock took three days to catch the lion that had really escaped. He pulled it out of another sewer during the night.

*A rumour is a story which is not true. It is passed on from one person to another.
*A sewer is a big underground drain.

Look at the story again

Answer in sentences:
1 What frightened the people at the fair?
2 Who was really making all the noise in the sewer?
3 Why was the circus full up after the lion escaped?
4 Why did Mr Bostock try to catch the lion?
5 Where did he find the lion that really escaped?

Let's talk about telling lies

1 Do you think Mr Bostock let a lion loose on purpose? Why?
2 Mr Bostock told a lie to all the people. Do you think he was right to pretend he had captured the lion?
3 Are there times when it is right to tell lies?
4 What do you say to your friends if they ask you about their new clothes or hairstyles? Do you always tell the truth?

A circus story

Mr Bostock is pleased that his circus was filled with people who have come to see the lion. Write what he says before the lion comes into the ring.
Begin: 'Ladies and gentlemen, now for the great moment of our show . . .' Mr Bostock could make up a story to show how fierce the lion was. He could tell people of the great struggle he had to 'capture' it.

Rumours

Imagine that Mr Bostock wanted to start rumours that would make people come to his circus. Make up two rumours he could start. Remember that people are interested in danger.

10 Late night horror

There are some nights we stay up late
To watch the TV horror show.
We see the vampire meet its fate
Or werewolves hunting in the snow.
We watch the mummy come to life
Or towns attacked by red-eyed rats
Or there's a madman with a knife;
– A haunted house with fluttering bats,
Things made of slime, a creeping hand,
A pool of blood, a talking head,
A torture room, a foggy land
Where live the green-faced, walking dead.

And then, when we switch off the set,
We laugh and say that it was wet.

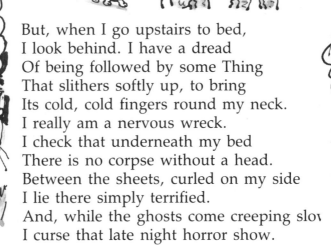

But, when I go upstairs to bed,
I look behind. I have a dread
Of being followed by some Thing
That slithers softly up, to bring
Its cold, cold fingers round my neck.
I really am a nervous wreck.
I check that underneath my bed
There is no corpse without a head.
Between the sheets, curled on my side
I lie there simply terrified.
And, while the ghosts come creeping slow
I curse that late night horror show.

22

Make a list

What are the horrors in the TV show? Write them all down.

Sentence endings

Finish these sentences. They need not be about the poem.
1 The vampire bit ....
2 The werewolf chased ....
3 A thousand rats swarmed ....
4 The creeping hand ....
5 The most frightening part was ......

Making sentences

Write this out in four sentences. Put in four capital letters and four full-stops:

the hand came through the window it had only three fingers the nails were long and purple it seemed to be looking for something

Capital letters

The names of films have capital letters. Write out these film titles beginning each word with a capital letter:

the mummy's hand   walking dead vampire's revenge

Write in sentences

1 Use each of these words in a 'creepy' sentence of your own:

horror   haunted   torture   nervous

2 Write five sentences about a haunted house. It could be a house near you.
3 Imagine you are baby-sitting and there is a loud rap on the window. Write four sentences about what happens next.

Drawing

Draw a picture from the poem.

Let's talk about horror!

1 Have you ever seen a horror film? What was it about?
2 What things frighten you most in films?
3 Have you ever felt like the writer of the poem?

23

11 Drop cakes

Recipe

These can be made in the kitchen at home or when camping. They taste best when eaten warm from the pan. To make 16 to 18 cakes you will need these things:

½ pound or 225 grammes of ordinary, plain flour
1 teaspoonful of baking powder.
2 eggs
about a cupful of milk

Mix all these together. Add a little milk at a time. Make a paste which is not so runny that it drips off a spoon. It mustn't be so stiff that it sticks to a spoon without running at all. Then, if you like currants, add:

1 cupful of currants

Mix the currants so that they are well spread in the mixture.

Then heat a frying pan. Take:

1 tablespoonful of oil

Pour the oil into the frying pan. Don't get the oil so hot that it smokes. It is hot enough when a little drop of the mixture put in the pan begins to sizzle and fry.

Put in small dollops of the mixture. A tablespoonful is about right. Don't put too many in the pan at once. When they are firm enough, turn them over. Fry until they are just crisp and brown on both sides. When you think they are ready, take one out. Let it cool for a moment. Then bite into it. If it is firm all through, the cakes are ready. If it is still a bit runny in the middle, fry the cakes a little longer.

Put in a little more oil, and fry the next spoonfuls of mixture. Do this again until all the mixture is used up.

True or false?

Look at the recipe again. Then write down the sentences that are true.

1 Half a pound of flour, or 225 grammes, is needed to make 26 to 38 cakes.
2 With half a pound of flour you can make 16 to 18 cakes.
3 Add the milk a little at a time.
4 Put one teaspoonful of oil in the frying pan.
5 Heat the oil until it smokes.
6 Fry the cakes a few at a time.

Food

Match up these foods with the country they came from. If you don't know some of them, you can find them in a dictionary.

spaghetti   Spain
Edam cheese   Holland
curry   Britain
fish and chips   China
paella   Greece
chop suey   America
baklava   India
Kentucky fried chicken Italy

Write in sentences

In three sentences, write out the strangest recipe you can think of. It could be for something you would hate to eat. It could be for fly-cakes, or caterpillar soup, or worm hamburgers.

Let's talk about cooking

Imagine you are left alone in the house for the weekend. You have to make two breakfasts, two midday meals and two evening meals. You can't go out and buy take-aways. What will you make? List your menus. Compare yours with the others. Who has the best menu in the class? Who has picked the most unhealthy foods? Who is the best cook?

12 Catching Rufus

Cast

Mum Dad Joel Leonora Rufus, a small, white, crafty dog

Scene: Outside the house

Mum	Right. Everything is packed. Seaside, here we come.
Dad	Let's get Rufus down to the kennels.
Leonora	He's hiding in the bush. He saw you pack the car. Rufus!
Rufus	Woof.
Leonora	That's his friendly bark. He'll be out in a minute.
Dad	We've only got a minute. Come on, you stupid animal.
Rufus	Woof, woof, *wooooof*.
Leonora	Now you've upset him.
Mum	Joel, what are you doing? You'll tear your clothes.
Joel	If a dog can get in this bush, so can a boy. Ow!
Mum	What's the matter?
Joel	I'm stuck and I've scratched my face.
Rufus	Grr! Grr!
Leonora	Now you've really got Rufus mad. He'll stay there all day.
Dad	I'll set fire to the bush and smoke him out.
Rufus	Grr! GRR! WOOF!
Dad	I'll woof you, you stupid animal.
Leonora	Dad, keep out.
Mum	Too late Leonora. Now Dad's got himself stuck.
Dad	Help me out of this damn bush. Hurry up, woman. I'm suffering.
Joel	And me!
Rufus	WOOF WOOF . . . woof . . . woof . . .
Joel	Now he's run off. He waited until we were all busy. He's too clever by half.
Leonora	He's cleverer than you. That doesn't take much. If you hadn't gone into the bush . . .
Mum	Oh, shut up. We'll never get off. Dad, we'll have to take him with us.
Dad	That dog gets his own way every time.
Leonora	Can I go and tell him he can come?
Dad	Oh, all right. None of us will get there if he doesn't, I suppose.

Leonora	(*shouts*) Rufus, you can come on holiday. So come out, wherever you are.
Rufus	Woof.
Mum	Here he comes. He heard what we were saying. He is clever.
Dad	Sometimes I don't think he's a dog at all but a human being with four legs that woofs.
Mum	Come on, then. Let's get going.

How clever are animals?

Put these six animals in order of cleverness. Start with the one you think is the most clever. End with the one you think is the most stupid.

cat fox sheep elephant donkey dog

Try to give a reason for your choice. Some of these ideas about animals might help you.

1 One animal is good at tricks.
2 One is often crafty in animal stories.
3 One always follows the others.
4 One is said to be good at remembering.
5 We use one of the animals' names to say somebody is stupid.
6 One is clever at finding the best place to lie down, and is crafty at stealing.

Groups of animals

Fill in the missing word in these lines. Choose it from the list below.

a _____ of cows   a _____ of geese
a _____ of sheep   a _____ of bees
a _____ of fish

shoal gaggle swarm herd flock

Write in sentences

1 Rufus was a clever dog. Write four sentences about something clever or very stupid that an animal you know has done.
2 This is how a toad might feel about a human:

The human is a very ugly animal. He has only two legs. His eyes don't bulge out nicely. He can't croak at all. He feels all dry, not nice and moist. He even has to learn to swim.

Write five sentences about how a giraffe or an elephant might feel about a human.

13 Kevin keeps fit

Kevin lived alone in a small house. He wanted to get fit.
It was a windy, winter night, but he went jogging. He
got back home very hot and tired. So he ran a bath and
got in. The hot water was splendid.

Then the front door bell rang. Kevin swore. It rang
again. He got out of the bath. He wrapped a towel round
himself and ran downstairs. He opened the front door.
There was no one there. He swore again. Someone must
have rung his bell for a joke. He stepped outside to look.
He could see two boys running away. He shouted angrily
but they did not stop. Kevin shivered.

The wind blew more strongly and the front door
slammed shut behind Kevin. He stared at it. He couldn't
believe it. He jogged quickly up and down on the step,
thinking. His towel fell off as some people came along,
talking. Kevin hid behind a bush. The people went away.
He grabbed his towel and wrapped it round himself
again. Then he jogged to the back of the house. The back
door was locked. So were all the back windows.

He jogged round the house, trying all the windows.
They were all locked. At last he charged at the front
door. He hurt his shoulder and the door stayed locked.
He charged at the back door. That didn't open, either.
He thought he would freeze to death.

In the end he broke a window with a stone and
climbed through. He ran up the stairs, shivering. He
jumped into the bath but the water was almost cold. He
jumped out and quickly put on his tracksuit and shoes.
The wind was blowing in through the broken window
and the house was cold. There was only one way to get
warm again. Kevin ran out of the house. He jogged
round the park and through the streets. He was warm
when he got back. But he was very tired.

Next night, Kevin mended the window. He sat next to
the fire and watched TV. No more jogging for me, he
thought.

Look at the story again

Find a sentence in the story to answer each of these.
1 Where did Kevin live?
2 Why did his door bell ring?
3 What happened when Kevin was locked out and people came along?
4 How did he get back into the house?
5 What did he do after he mended the window?

Missing letters

The same two letters are missing from each of these words. Write out each sentence, spelling the words correctly.
1 He ran downst__rs.
2 They went on the dodgems at the f__r.
3 She bought a red p__r of shoes.
4 He was always combing his h__r.
5 Grandad sat in his old ch__r.

Find the rhymes

Which word in the story rhymes with each of these?

logging   rain   cunning   growing
walking   docked   barged   boulder

Make a list

List three kinds of exercise that will keep you fit. List four kinds of food that are good for your health. List four things that are not good for your health.

Let's talk about keeping fit

Compare your lists with the others in the class. How do you keep fit? What happens when people don't keep fit?

14 The old guitar

Not many people liked Joanne. She was small, she always looked untidy, and she wasn't good at anything. At home, she had to look after her two small brothers when her mother went out to work. No one knew the family very well. Joanne's dad had left home long ago, and they didn't talk to the neighbours.

One day Joanne was at the market. Her mother had sent her, to pick out some of the fruit thrown away by the market traders. From behind one stall she heard someone crying. She found an old woman holding a dog in her arms. Joanne asked what was the matter.

'My dog is very ill and cannot walk,' cried the old woman. 'He is too heavy for me to carry home. I've been here for hours, but nobody takes any notice.'

'I'll help you,' said Joanne. She picked up the dog. It was very heavy, but she could just manage. The old lady followed her slowly.

When they got to the old lady's flat, she said, 'I must give you something, my dear.'

'Oh, no,' said Joanne. 'I was glad to help.'

But the old lady had already opened a big cupboard under the sink. She took out an old, battered guitar, and pushed it into Joanne's arms.

Joanne thanked the old lady and ran home with the guitar. She strummed the strings. They made a wonderful sound. To her surprise, she found she could play any tune she wanted. The guitar almost seemed to play itself.

Joanne took the guitar to school next day.
'What a rubbish guitar!' said Tom.
'It's not electric. It can't be any good,' said Annie.
'Only good for firewood,' laughed John. 'I bet you can't play a note!'

Joanne strummed the guitar. Then she played a hit number they all knew. The children were amazed. Joanne played tune after tune for them, and Annie sang the words.

30

Joanne and Annie soon became good friends. They sang and played together. Joanne was happy, and she began to do better in her school work. But she didn't forget her old lady. After a few weeks she went round to thank her again.

When she got there, the flat was boarded up. Nobody knew about an old lady. The place had been empty for years, they told her.

Missing letters

Complete the names of these musical instruments:

gu_ _ _ _   dr_ _   pi_ _ _   or_ _ _
tr_ _ _ _ _   saxo_ _ _ _ _

Capital letters

Make a list of your four favourite pop groups or bands. Use capital letters at the start of each word.

Look at the story again

Answer in sentences:
1 How many children were there in Joanne's family?
2 Why was Joanne at the market?
3 Why was the old lady holding the dog?
4 What words describe the guitar?
5 Why do you think Joanne could play the guitar?
6 What was the mystery of the old lady's flat?

Spelling

Use each of these spellings in a sentence of your own:

something surprise successful anything cupboard popular everything

Make a list

What things do you own that are very old but you like a lot?

Write a story

Write a story called *The Old Picture* or *The Old Book* or *The Old House*.

Let's talk about musical instruments

1 Which do you like best? Why?
2 Which would you like to play?
3 What is the best way to learn?

15 Fire!

It was a winter's night. Wayne was working on his motor bike. He was going to respray the petrol tank. It was freezing in the shed. So he decided to take the tank into the house. There was no one to stop him. His mother and father were out.

He spread a newspaper in front of the fire in the living room. He carried the tank in and put it on the newspaper. Then he went back to the shed for the rest of the things he needed.

He should have been much more careful. There was a drop or two of petrol left in the tank. That made it a time bomb. Fumes from the petrol reached the open fire. There was a sudden *whoosh*! Flames filled the room. In seconds there were small fires everywhere, quickly growing into bigger fires.

Luckily Wayne did not panic. He rang the fire brigade. But the fire did a lot of damage before it was put out.

There are tens of thousands of fires in homes in Britain every year. Last year about 1,000 people died in these fires. Nearly 8,000 people were injured.

It is much easier to prevent fires than to put them out. There are certain things you can do to stop a fire happening in a house.

Children playing with matches can start fires. So don't leave matches where small children can get hold of them. People who fall asleep while smoking can cause fires. See that all cigarettes are put out properly. Don't smoke in bed. There are chip pan fires, too. Don't fill a chip pan too full of fat. Don't turn the heat up too high. And don't go away and leave a hot chip pan unwatched. There are electrical fires. Don't have too many plugs on one socket. Don't use a plug if you think it may be faulty. Unplug all electric plugs when they are not being used.

Dangerous fires can start at night. Before you go to bed, put a guard in front of any open fires. Unplug all electric plugs. As you go upstairs close all the doors.

Look at the story again

Answer these questions in sentences of your own.

1 What made the petrol tank so dangerous in the house?
2 What was the right thing Wayne did when the fire started?
3 How many fires in the home are there in Britain every year?
4 What two things should you *not* do with electrical plugs?
5 Why should you close the doors in a house before going to bed?

Emergency One

What number do you dial for these?

Fire   Coastguard   Police   Lifeboat
Ambulance   Rescue

Emergency Two

1 What four things should you say when this number answers?
2 Write out what you think you should do. Check that you are right in a telephone directory.

Let's talk about safety in sport

1 Choose one of the following:

   swimming   cycling   canoeing
   walking in rough country
   any other sport

2 Write a list of safety 'do's' and 'don'ts' for your sport. Put the most important safety rule first, the second most important second and so on.
3 Compare your list with others in the class who have chosen the same sport.
4 Have any safety rules been missed out? Are the lists in the right order of importance? Who has made the most sensible list?

16 Tina's fear

Tina's parents had gone out for the evening. She was eleven.Her dad said she was far too old to have a baby-sitter. Tina did not like to say she was scared to be in the house on her own.

In the daytime Tina's house was friendly. At night, if she was on her own, it was full of dangerous places. There were huge spiders waiting for her in the bathroom. There was a ghost under the stairs. The ghost squeaked and whispered when she climbed the stairs. There was a rat with red eyes and crooked yellow teeth in the kitchen. The only safe place was in the lounge.

Tina sat in the lounge and talked to Wilson. Wilson was an old and bad-tempered cat in the daytime. At night when Tina was on her own, Wilson became her best friend. Her only friend. He could scratch and bite anybody who broke into the house. Well, Tina hoped so.

The telephone rang. Tina put her fingers to her ears and counted loudly up to fifty. This was usually long enough to stop the telephone ringing. Of course she could not answer it. It was on a table under the stairs, just next to the ghost.

That night the telephone rang six times. Sometimes it rang so long that Tina had to count fifty twice before it shut up.

At last Tina heard the car coming into the drive. She rushed upstairs past the ghost. Of course he had hidden himself now her parents were home. She got into bed and pretended to be asleep. Soon she was really asleep.

As she lay in bed the next morning she heard the telephone again. She heard her dad saying, 'Only Tina. She was asleep . . . Six times? Well, when she's asleep you have as much chance of waking the dead.'

'Who was it, dear?' Tina heard her mum asking.

'Old Carter. He wanted us to go round tonight to his dinner-party – somebody dropped out. He tried to leave a message last night. Of course, Tina didn't hear the phone. He's got somebody else now, thank heavens. He wanted to show us his boring holiday slides.'

Tina smiled and turned over in her bed. The house would be friendly tonight.

Look at the story again

Finish these sentences in your own words.

1 Tina did not have a baby-sitter because ….
2 Tina hoped that if a burglar came Wilson would ….
3 When the telephone rang Tina ….
4 Tina could not answer the telephone because ….
5 When Tina heard her parents' car she ….
6 Tina's dad thought she never answered the telephone because ..
7 Mr Carter kept ringing to ask Tina's dad ….
8 Tina's dad was pleased she had not answered the phone because he did not want ….

Let's talk about being afraid

1 Tina did not like to tell her parents she was afraid. Write down three things you are afraid of. These suggestions might help you decide:

– having to climb up a high ladder.
– being told off at school.
– having to play games you hate.
– animals such as spiders, rats, snakes.
– walking home in the dark by yourself.
– being caught doing wrong by your parents.

Compare your fears with others in the class.

2 Talk about people's silly fears. For instance, if you fell off a high ladder you would hurt yourself, but can a spider hurt you?

Imagining things

1 What three things does Tina imagine are in her house when she is on her own?
2 Where does she think each one is?

17 Lights out

Cast

The Donson family: Dad Mum Grandad
George (aged 11) Suzie (aged 17)

*Scene: Dad and George are watching TV. Mum is doing a
crossword. Grandad is asleep. Suzie is ironing a dress.
Suddenly all the lights in the house go out.*

Mum	That's done it. The lights have gone out.
Dad	Get some candles. It must be a power cut.
Mum	We haven't any.
Dad	George, get your torch.
George	It's no use. The battery's flat.
Dad	Get Grandad's matches.
Mum	He's sitting on them.
Dad	Well put your hand under him and pull them out.
Mum	I can't see him.
Dad	Feel round for him then.
Suzie	Ouch! I've burnt my fingers. Where are the plasters?
Mum	Upstairs. You can light the way with one of Grandad's matches when I get them.
Grandad	What! Eh! Get off!
Mum	It's only me. The lights have gone out. We need your matches.
Grandad	They're with my pipe on the kitchen table.
Dad	I'll go and feel for them. I'll put the kettle on while I'm there. We'll make a cup of tea.
George	What will you boil the water with? Your hot breath?
Grandad	The fire's gone out.
George	Now we'll either die of cold, thirst or boredom.
Mum	Don't moan. We'll have a family talk. We never talk to each other. What shall we talk about?
Dad	Why you didn't buy any candles?
George	Don't you two quarrel. Let's play a game.
Suzie	Blind Man's Buff, I suppose.
Mum	We'll all go to bed. Then we won't quarrel.
George	Dad, look out of the window.
Dad	Well, would you believe it. The lights are all on down the road. It must be a fuse . . .

Make a list

Write down all the things the Donson family could not use when their electricity went off.

Write in sentences

Write six sentences saying what would happen if there was no electricity in your house.

Exclamations!

When Mrs Donson woke Grandad, he said: 'What! Eh! Get off!'
We all shout out if we are surprised or frightened. An exclamation mark shows how the words are being said – with fear, surprise, anger, happiness.
Write what you might say just after these things happened:
1 A big dog jumped on you.
2 You heard you had won a big sum of money or passed a hard exam.
3 A bird messed on your head.
4 A friend jumped out at you from behind a corner.

Before you start, check how the exclamation marks in Grandad's sentence are used.

Drawing

Put one hand over your eyes, so you cannot see your writing book or paper. Now draw a plan of your classroom. Put in doors, windows, desks, tables and cupboards. Now take your hand away from your eyes. What does your plan look like?

Adverts

Look at this advert from a torch manufacturer:

BEWARE THE POWER CUT
Don't be caught in the dark this winter

Always have a
BEAMGLOW
handy

Lights up your life on the darkest of nights

Make your own adverts for gas fires, oil fires, and gas cookers.

18 Be careful

This is a true story. Carol had seventeen pounds for her holiday. She kept it in an old brown jug on a shelf in her bedroom. One day she found the jug empty. Nobody knew where it had gone. There was no sign that the house had been broken into. Nothing else was missing. The doors were always locked and the windows shut when everybody was out. In the end Carol's dad gave her another seventeen pounds. She put it in the jug. Two days later it was gone. This time, Carol's dad rang the police.

Two policemen came that night. They looked round outside the house and in the garage. One said to Carol's dad, 'Either under that stone, or under the big tin on the garage shelf.'
Carol's dad didn't understand. He asked the policeman what he meant.

'I'm guessing where you hide your key when you go out,' said the policeman.
'We always hide it under the tin,' said Carol's dad.
'If I can guess, so can a thief,' said the policeman.

Carol suddenly remembered something. 'There was a boy who came down the passage to our back door last week,' she said. 'I was ill that day, so I was off school. I saw him through the window.'
'What happened?' asked the policeman.
'When he saw me, he just turned round and went away. I thought he had made a mistake and called at the wrong house. I forgot all about it.'
The policeman wrote down Carol's description of the boy. The police knew who he was. He had just come out of a detention centre. He had been caught stealing six times before that. He always took money or jewels.

The police soon caught the boy. He admitted stealing Carol's money. He was sent to a detention centre for two weeks. After he came out, he had to pay Carol back.

Carol's statement

The policeman asked Carol seven questions. He then made this statement from her answers:

On Tuesday, the 11th of June at 2 p.m. I was sitting in the kitchen reading when I heard footsteps. I looked up and saw a boy walking down the passage. When he saw me he turned and walked away. He was wearing jeans and a red T-shirt. He had long, fair curly hair and was tall and thin. I did not mention this to my parents because I thought he had just gone to the wrong house and he knew it was wrong when he saw me.

What questions do you think the policeman asked Carol? Write them down.

Warnings

Make a notice to warn people not to leave keys where thieves can find them. Your notice can be all words or you can add a drawing – your thief could be watching someone hide a key under a stone.

Let's talk about crime

1 Put the list of crimes below in order of seriousness – the most serious first, the least serious last.
   – a boy of twelve steals £2 worth of sweets from a shop.
   – a man is found drunk while driving his car.
   – a boy of twelve steals £2 from an old lady's purse.
   – a youth of 19 throws a dart at a rival supporter at a football match.
   – a man drives 50 miles an hour in a 30 mile limit.
   – a lady drowns her dog in the river because she can't afford to feed it any more.
2 Now list the punishments you think should be given for each crime.
3 Compare your lists with others in the class. Talk about some of these points:
   – how much is stolen?
   – where is it stolen from?
   – what is worse, to steal or to hurt someone?

19 Wonder man

Imagine four or five houses placed one on top of another. That is about the height of Niagara Falls. At Niagara the water falls nearly 50 metres into a whirlpool. The Falls are about 300 metres wide. Blondin walked across the Falls – several times.

Blondin was a Frenchman. His real name was Gravelet. He was born in 1824. When he was five years old, his parents sent him to train as an acrobat. Six months later he made his first public appearance. He was good enough to have his name on the poster. He was called 'The Little Wonder'.

He first crossed Niagara in 1859. The tightrope he used was nearly 336 metres long. It took him twenty minutes to walk from one side of the Falls to the other side. Halfway across he stopped and let down a rope. Far below him, in the rough water at the foot of the Falls, a rescue boat was waiting. People on the boat tied a bottle and a glass to Blondin's rope. He pulled it up, opened the bottle and filled his glass. Then he drank a toast to the thousands of people watching him. He was standing on one leg on the tightrope at the time.

Next time, he made the crossing more difficult. He walked the tightrope across the Falls blindfold. Then he pushed a man in a wheelbarrow all the way across. He carried a man across on his back. Then he walked across on a pair of stilts. On his next trip he stopped halfway to cook and eat a snack.

The act made Blondin world famous. It also made him very rich. He came to live in Britain. But he did not stop working. Three years after walking across Niagara, he walked an even higher tightrope.

That was at the Crystal Palace. On a tightrope nearly 60 metres above the ground, he walked across on stilts. Then he turned somersaults on the rope. He did that in a thunderstorm.

He went on risking death for years. Even when he was over seventy, he was still walking the high rope. He died quietly in bed in London in 1897 just before his seventy-third birthday.

Look at the story again

1 How high in metres is Niagara Falls?
2 When did Blondin first start acting in public?
3 Where did Blondin walk an even higher tightrope than the one at Niagara?
4 Which, do you think, was the most difficult or dangerous trick he did?

Words

All these words are in the story. From the meanings given here, find the words. Write each one down. The first two letters will help you.
1 This is like a tiny cart with one wheel. It is a wh_____.
2 This is water swirling round and round and round. It is a wh_____.
3 This is a person who does tricks on a trapeze or tightrope. It is an ac_____.
4 This is a small meal. It is a sn___.
5 If something is very hard to do, it is di_____.

Numbers

Write these numbers out in words:

50   300   8   25   41

Write these numbers out in figures:

two hundred and ten   ninety-eight four hundred and seven eighty-eight

Write in sentences

What was the most interesting trick you ever saw? Was it in public or on television? Was it dangerous? Was it difficult? Was it interesting because it was clever?
Write five or six sentences about it.
1 Say who did the trick, where you saw it and what happened.
2 Were you interested because it was a bit frightening?
3 Did you admire the person performing the trick?
4 Was it interesting because you did not know how the trick was done?

20 Colour blind

Cast

Sara Yasmin Javed Mr Smith

Scene 1: The school yard

Sara	There's something odd about the new art teacher.
Yasmin	Yes, there's something about his eyes I don't like.
Javed	What rubbish! He's just another boring teacher. Nothing odder about him than any other teacher.
Sara	I just get that feeling. I hate going to art.
Yasmin	We have an art lesson this afternoon.

Scene 2: The art room

Mr Smith	You have painted a very nice picture, Sara, but the colours are a little odd, don't you think?
Sara	No.
Mr Smith	Why have you made the grass all green.
Sara	Grass is green.
Mr Smith	Ah, yes, you are quite right. But don't you see any other colours in it? You can have many colours in a tree, too.

Scene 3: The school yard

Sara	He is odd. He doesn't think grass should be green. What does he want it to be? Pink I suppose.
Javed	He just meant there are yellows and browns in grass.
Sara	No, it was something more than that. I don't like him.
Yasmin	He could be colour blind.
Sara	What? A colour blind art teacher?
Yasmin	He started to put purple on my sun. Then he changed his mind and said it should be orange.
Sara	You don't expect that from an art teacher.
Yasmin	There is a mystery about him.
Sara	Yes, I get a feeling that he is not from this world.

Finish the play

What do you think happens next? How does it all end? Think it over first. These questions will help you. Answer in sentences.

1 Where could the strange art teacher come from?
2 What made Sara worry about him?
3 What does red look like to a person who is colour blind?
4 Could there be any other reason why the strange teacher is there?

Colours

1 What colours can you see in trees? Make a list.
2 What are the colours of the rainbow? Make a list.
3 What colours do you like to dress in? What colour would you like your hair to be?

Silly sentences

Here is a silly sentence: I took my pink dog into the yellow river. Write three sentences using colours in a silly way.

Let's talk about aliens from outer space

Why do you think creatures from outer space might want to take over the Earth?

Spelling

What words rhyme with *green*. Write five *ee* words in one column and five *ea* words in another, like this:

ee	ea
been	clean
seen	beam

Write in sentences

Write four sentences about a teacher who has something odd about him or her. You could begin: One day an odd teacher came to our school . . .

21 Secret codes

On this page, there are some messages in secret codes. For each code, copy out the alphabet first. Then write out your code alphabet underneath. You could use a different colour for this. This will help you match the code letters with the real ones, and find out the secret messages.

In the first two messages B has been used instead of A, and C instead of B and so on:

Alphabet A B C D E F G H I J K L M N O P Q R S T U V W X Y Z
Code   B C D E F etc.

Message 1 UIF TFDSFU NFTTBHF JT JO B UJO UXP NFUSFT GSPN UIF PME PBL USFF CZ UIF MFGU IBOE HBUF QPTU

Message 2 UIF TFDSFU BHFOU XJMM NFFU ZPV CZ UIF BCD DJOFNB IF XJMM XFBS B SFE SPTF

In the next two messages Z has been used instead of A, A has been used instead of B, B instead of C and so on:

Alphabet A B C D E F G H I J K L M N O P Q R S T U V W X Y Z
Code   Z A B C D E F etc.

Message 3 Z GDKHBNOSDQ VHKK KZMC VHSG OZQBDK HM SGD UZKKDX AX SGD BZMZK AQHCFD

Message 4 XNTQ CHRFTHRD HR HM KDES KTFFZFD ANW 873 ZS JHMFR BQNRR RSZSHNM

In the next message the word 'the' is VJG. What is the code?

Alphabet A B C D E F G H I J K L M N O P Q R S T U V W X Y Z
Code   G   J   V

Message 5 AQW ECP IGV AQWT UGETGV VCRG HTQO VJG UYGGVUJQR CUM HQT C TGF NQNNA

44

Write in code

1 Send this message in the code used in messages 1 and 2 on page 44:

    Meet me by the old windmill at midnight.

2 Send this message in the code used in messages 3 and 4:

    You will see a blind man by the pillar box in the High Street. Give him the letter.

3 Send this message in the code used in message 5:

    You will find the tape stuck under the third table from the door in Fred's Cafe.

    Make up a code. Write a short message. Give it to a friend to solve.

    Make up a picture code. Here is a start for you:

Alphabet	A	B	C	D
Code		⊞	△	⊗

Write in sentences

Describe how you followed a man you thought was a spy down your street or road. Write five sentences.

Make a list

Make a list of six hiding places where you could hide a secret video.

Alphabetical order

Put these words into alphabetical order:

bugging **t**ape **v**ideo **p**oison **r**adio **s**ecret **c**ode **d**isguise **a**gent **m**essage

Making sentences

Write this in six sentences. Use six capital letters and six full-stops:

i went down the road a man was standing at the corner his hat was turned down over his face there was a car opposite him i did not like the look of his stick it could be a gun

Let's talk about spies

1 Why do countries have spies?
2 What do spies do?
3 What happens if spies are caught?

22 A fishy story

The day by the sea was a hot one. The Morris family had come down from London to Sussex for a holiday. This was their first day. They were going to have a picnic on Wittering beach.

Mick and Jackie, the two children, quickly undressed. They ran splashing into the sea. 'Oh! It's lovely and warm!' they cried. 'You must come in too.'

'Are you going in, Dad?' asked Mrs Morris.

Mr Morris grunted from behind his copy of the *Sun*, 'No fear!'

'Well, I am,' she said. She changed under a beach towel. She giggled as she tip-toed across some pebbles to the water. 'Oh, it is warm!' she cried. 'Dad, you must come in!'

Mr Morris rolled up his trousers and took his boots off. This was as far as he would go.

But soon three dripping bodies were round him. 'You must come in, Dad.'

'I've brought your costume,' giggled Mrs Morris.

'I thought we came for some peace and quiet. Oh, all right then.' He changed under the *Sun*.

What happened next surprised the children. Mr Morris ran over the sand into the water and dived into a wave.

He came up spluttering. The family could not make out what he was saying for a moment. Slowly it became clear.

'I've lost me teeth! I've lost me teeth!'

The family spent the rest of the day trying to find the teeth. The water got deeper as the tide came in. They did not eat till after the tide went out again.

Mr Morris was furious. 'It's all your fault,' he said to the others. He spoke as though his mouth was full of wet lettuce.

Later, the family had chicken legs and crisps. All Mr Morris could manage was the jelly.

He was fitted up with a pair of teeth next day by a grumpy dentist. But they did not fit well and he complained to the family all week.

On the last day of the holiday Mr Morris went fishing on the pier. He quickly landed the largest fish he had ever caught. When he pulled out the hook, he was amazed. Out popped a pair of false teeth. They looked like his lost teeth. He put them in. They were very salty. But they were his!

Write in sentences

Describe these in one sentence:
1 A wave coming in and slowly knocking over a sandcastle.
2 How you feel when you first dive, swim or paddle in cold water.
3 How you feel walking over stones or pebbles on a beach.

What is the difference?

Write each word from these pairs in a sentence of your own:

peer pier   the sun the *Sun*
tied tide   pear pair   court caught

Make a list

1 Make a list of things you need to take for a beach picnic. Divide them into things to eat and other things (like cups and chairs).
2 Make a list of 'spare parts' you can have for the body.

Let's talk about fish stories

1 Have you heard any other stories of things found in a fish?
2 What fish might have the most things in it?
3 What man was swallowed by a whale in the Bible story? Is it possible?

Self-marking record card

COPY THIS INTO YOUR BOOK. DO NOT MARK THIS BOOK.

I have done these sections (cross off):

1 2 3 4 5 6 7 8 9 10 11 12 13 14 15 16 17 18 19
20 21 22

My best work was on sections: _____

I have written _____ stories. (Write in how many.)

I have written _____ plays.

I have written _____ poems.

I CAN/CANNOT send a message in code.
I am GOOD/NOT SO GOOD at making lists.
I put a capital letter at the start of sentences ALWAYS/SOMETIMES/NEVER.
I put a full-stop at the end of sentences ALWAYS/SOMETIMES/NEVER.
I remember to put the question mark at the end of questions
ALWAYS/SOMETIMES/NEVER.

I can now spell these words (cross off):

a lot does goes clothes until coming tried frightened heard
really

I know my alphabet. YES/NO.
I can find a word in a dictionary SOMETIMES/ALWAYS.
I DO/DO NOT mix up small and capital letters in my writing.

I use capital letters for these things (cross off):

names of people nicknames pets' names towns pop groups films

I can pick out sentences that are true. YES/NO.

I can spot a rhyme. YES/NO.

I found it HARD/EASY to talk about things in this book.